HERE TODAY
Zen Inspired Poetry

Here Today

Zen Inspired Poetry

by KEN NOYLE

CHARLES E. TUTTLE CO.: PUBLISHERS
Rutland, Vermont & Tokyo, Japan

Representatives

For Continental Europe:
BOXERBOOKS, INC., *Zurich*

For the British Isles:
PRENTICE-HALL INTERNATIONAL, INC., *London*

For Australasia:
PAUL FLESCH & CO., PTY. LTD., *Melbourne*

For Canada:
M. G. HURTIG LTD., *Edmonton*

Published by the Charles E. Tuttle Company, Inc.
of Rutland, Vermont & Tokyo, Japan
with editorial offices at Suido 1-chome, 2-6, Bunkyo-ku, Tokyo

© *1969 by Charles E. Tuttle Company, Inc.*

Library of Congress Catalog Card No. 69-19609

Standard Book No. 8048 0244-0

First edition, 1969
Second printing, 1970

PRINTED IN JAPAN

FOR CHERRY—
NOW SHE'S ALMOST A WOMAN.

FOR YOKO—
BECAUSE SHE'S A WOMAN.

FOR TOM KORZENIOWSKI—
WHO SUFFERED EVERY COMMA.

FOR ANDRE CALABUIG—
FOR A THOUSAND THINGS,
INCLUDING PUBLISHING MY FIRST BOOK.

TABLE OF CONTENTS

INTRODUCTION

My fat ego purred over the critiques of my last collection, *Gone Tomorrow*. But then my big, thin, cowardly streak whispered, "Quit while you're ahead." For a poet is lucky, damned lucky, to be published and actually read by old-nameless-face—the public—and then, to even be noticed by the critics, let alone be honored by their scalpels, is something else again.

And, I said to me, just what is a poet? I don't look like a poet; I certainly don't play golf like a poet; my appetites are far from ascetic and I don't look at every sunrise and emote great globs of profundity. The Beatles are, I think, poets of great dimension and, of course, Robert Frost is a spine tingler. But then John D. McDonald shapes sentences that shiver me the same way.

I know a poet is supposed to tell the truth and this, to tell the truth, I try to do, except in a couple of my poems (or whatever you call them). I just write whatever comes into my mind, come what may, as it flows, uncorrected, uncontrived—except for a couple of exceptions, and even these don't start off that way.

Just what is truth? I believe it is a commodity as scarce today as love. Of course, there's cola truth—bottled and imbibed in every country, concocted from patent syrups, easily digested, frostily delicious, but causing thirst to come again too soon, while the real truth is often bitter, always strange tasting and quite intoxicating, bearing the labels of many vineyards of the mind and derived from the soils of uncountable existences; an acquired taste and, sometimes, an expensive one.

If I am indeed a poet, I can claim no poetic philosophy. Old Omar Khayyam has said it all and I would hate to be responsible to a mother who felt her child had succumbed to my amoral merriment. I draw God without a face and my views on sex would not gain the trust of a teeny-bopper's parents, and my refusal to believe that life is not as dull and difficult as some people make it will not endear me to the cabbages.

But, I threw this bottle into the sea, hoping the right one would fish it out—one who would not be disappointed by the words, but would have the knack of deciphering the spaces, of winkling the meat out of the periods, and hearing the intended silences. This, as well as the ability to add personal vibrations to the 12-point Bembo.

If you are such a one, welcome to my mind. If you care to ferret around in there and come up with something that twitches you, however little, then I'm glad I did it, and with the slightest encouragement from you, I'll do it again.

Ken Noyle

Tokyo, Japan

I Am

I am!
I am . . .
What a way to start a book.
Why do I open my mental fly
And expose myself to you?
Not for perversion, or the flagellation of my ego
With the knotted rope of self-confession.
No!
I start with I am!
Because I am!
I am . . .
Is the starting point of everyone and everything.
Right?
And I feel your "I am" will not accept me,
Or the things of which I burble
Until you sniff around a little
And decide what kind of "I am" I am!

I am what I am
Because I am,
And for no other rhyme or reason.
I've shaped myself for good or bad
On printed words and spoken words and whims and menus
And the hands of girls.
Colors have turned me like iron filings
Swung by a magnet!
Songs and seas and lonely nights
Have tuned me, honed me,
And the scars have left a rose tattoo
Not washed off by good advice or warnings.

I've made my bed and lie in it
Sometimes alone, and sometimes with another
Who knows that life is now!
For, was, was, was
And tomorrow is so damned far away
As to be a dream.
And now is life
And I am now!

You'll find, if nothing else,
I'll speak the truth.
Not that my truth is any truer,
But I won't write pretty words
In the hope of appealing to pretty minds.
And if you're one of those, forget it!
I've lost you here and now.

If you're still with me
I'll not bludgeon you with so-and-so's philosophy.
And if you're saddled with
A supermarket mind
And buy only name-brand thinking,
Adding the dry ingredients as directed on the box,
Until your Pillsbury-moist Philosocake
Merely requires your family recipe to ice it
And let you call it your own,
Then I guess I've lost you too.

You're still with me?
Good!
We "I ams" should stick together,
For alone, we are alone.
And together we are all the syllables of God!
And if, sometime, you have the gall

To put your random thoughts together in a book,
And you can find a Tuttle for your thoughts,
Count me in;
I'll blow a buck on you too!

So here I am,
Male
(Hurrah!)
Not white; not black;
But colored by the spraygun of days and nights . . .
A blending of shades
And bright blotches of experience
And the raw pigments of life itself.

I need no drugs to turn me on,
But I am hallucination prone,
For when I pop a thought into my skully skull,
I take the trip
And never count the cost.

Age?
23 above the navel
23 below . . .
I hear the whir of I.B.M.,
But I've fooled you by leaving out the zeros.
So forget it like I do,
Okay?

I live in Japan,
In a house cunningly fashioned;
Hot in summer, freezing in winter,
Built of wood and love and paper.

I shave my head . . .

You what?
I shave my head. Yes, everyday.
And from it grows . . . guess what?
Two long, quivering antennae (!!!)
Which
Retract on contact
With
People with big loud voices,
People with clammy limp hands,
Back slappers, religious hypocrites,
Fat priests in good restaurants,
Bigots, intolerant bulldozers,
People so fixed and rooted in their beliefs
That they have become cabbages,
Created in the image of the Almighty Cabbage
And his Brussel Sprout.
My anti-antennae
Do their snail impersonations
On meeting people who profit from other
People's misfortunes and weaknesses.
And I include God's businessmen, snug in
Their good suits and cozy
Convenient righteousness;
Also, with
Men who abuse women mentally or physically,
With people who lie to children,
And with those who not only use their power to destroy,
But find vindications for so doing.

That's torn one skin of the onion . . .
Now, what's next?
What was I?
I was, showbiz since I was 10.
One night stands and little schooling,

Split weeks and summer seasons;
Comedian,
Magician,
Following wars;
Audiences in jungles, deserts, ships,
And then clubs and
Lounges;
Radio, TV, ice shows, movies,
Circus, variety shows, fashion shows, and cabaret.
Knocked'em cold in 90 countries;
Wowed'em in Bangkok,
Killed'em in Calcutta,
Slayed'em in Kenya.
And now, I sneak in a show when time permits,
Shoot three dimensional photographs, try to
Write books and poetry,
And travel around the world,
Packing and unpacking my mind.

What else?
Well,
I cry easily . . .
Come now!
Confession is good for the soul,
But this is ridiculous.
No! No! No!
I don't mean that a torn hangnail
Reduces me to a slobbering heap. No!
I don't mean I actually ooze out fat, gooby tears,
But my cry mechanism reacts mostly
To parades with stirring music,
To children when they're so beautiful, but so impermanent;
To intense happiness, some music and poetry
And to love in all its fancy dresses.

I love women
And, of all my weaknesses,
This is the one for which I'm most thankful.
I love
Golden girls, cocooned in long black hair;
Windbells and shadowed shoji;
Warm girls; warm from the beach
Or glowing from snow;
Lost girls, finding and holding
And losing all in a moment;
Wise girls with secret tenderness,
Women's bodies and child-bright eyes;
Girls from many climes and times,
But not America!
Whether opportunity or cowardice stopped me
I couldn't say.
One ebony exception though, filled with bright,
Light wonder and a rare awareness:
The kind that separates the women from the girls.

Yes, I have known them
And kissed the taste of peppermint
And cocoa, early morning coffee
And the bitter sweet of gin.
I have wondered, I have thought,
And awakened in the night
Wishing the moment could last forever.
Or awakened in the morning
Wondering how soon the agony would end.

I have shared dawns and dusks
And midnights bright with flames.
I have dreamed dreams that came to life.
I have lived lives that came to dreams.

I have thirsted, quaffed,
And remained unquenched.
I have sipped . . . and found ambrosia
In a small chipped cup.

I have lied my share of lies
And believed my share of truth.
But to me
A woman is:
The most exciting, frustrating, unbelievable,
Joyful, thought provoking, funny,
Wonderful, and most necessary prank
The gods have ever played on me!
Heaven and Hell in one soft package,
Impossible to live with;
Impossible to live without.
Ole!

What else? I am untidy,
Except for when the urge takes me
To spring clean.
And then, a book out of place
Or a pencil's position disturbs me
And I must put it right.
A crooked picture bugs me,
But I can make a mess of a kitchen
Just pouring a glass of milk.
I play games with myself . . .
"Aha!" You say, "He masturbates!"
No, I do not!
Except perhaps with my ego . . .
No, I mean for instance
I play a game: That so-and-so
Will or will not happen if

I find my lost toothpaste cap before I count to 20.
And, sometimes, I count very
Slowly to give me an extra chance.
I rate girls by so many out of
Ten when I pass them in the street.

I am a believer.
I believe I can do what I want to do
And do it.
I live like a millionaire,
Although I'm not.
I'm careless of possessions
And zealous of friends.

My God has no name
And His house is mine,
For my religion is nameless.
Yet, I have one:
Part Zen and part an ardent belief
In the power of giving;
Believing that the more you give,
The more returns to you;
Be it love, hate, kindness
Or understanding.
But where
This great and boomeranging force
Originates or derives its power . . .
Search me!
And you'll find it
Somewhere deep inside.
That's why I search myself.
Zen!

I've studied most of

The Big God religions
And have come to the conclusion
That there's no conclusion.
And if you want your God lolling on a cloud
Or living in a tree or on a mountain top,
Good luck to you.

For all the wine and wafers
And all the nimble rosaries;
All the offerings, floral or bloody;
All the tempting, bribing, promising,
Prostitutions of the soul
Are all for one reason only:
The need to seek a reason.
For you, my friend,
Are alone in your decision, as am I,
Of the this-way or that-way of life.
The answer lies only in you,
For this is one subject that has no experts,
And you're as wise as anyone.
And if you call your answer
God
Or Dog
Or Ogd
Or Fred
Or Buddha
Or Shiva
Or Micky Mouse,
If you really believe that It-He-She helps you,
Go baby! Go!
For no one but no one can ever say you're wrong.

I am because I am!
Not just because someone died for me

Or stuck pins of passion into me
Or bathed me in mercy.
I am because so many people did so many things.
I am because I am,
And if I choose to believe that all the "I ams"
Are part of a whole,
With the power of good and evil,
I think that you'll agree!
This too could be a synonym for God.
So now we know each other a little more.
And if you look up from this page and think,
"This nut's a bit like me,"
Dear sir or madam as the case may be,
Believe me,
I am.

Entire of Itself

A woman is an island
Waiting to be explored,
But all the maps are out of date
And the one with the treasure
Marked clearly with a cross,
A myth.

Some islands welcome you ashore
And, as you stand there, castaway,
Wrapped in wonder,
You believe in your relief
That you can stay forever, contented in the sun.
But soon geography confines,
Beauty pales, beasts become a bore to hunt,
Climates too predictable,
And you'd welcome a storm
Or a damn great tidal wave
To wash you out to sea again.

Some islands offer no footholds,
But their mystery lures you on;
Ignoring the silences and shadows,
Believing this to be the silence of a Shangri-La.
And if you're not wary,
You sink into the sands of compromise,
And your cries for help
Are lost in the echoes of the bird's.

But, somewhere, there's an island for us all.
Somewhere out there, off the coast of everyday,

Torrid or tender,
With sustenance for the body
And inspirations blowing in the wind,
With intriguing trails in great profusion,
Inviting exploration,
Rewarding with sights and sounds so rare
That you become alive again
Each time you die a little.

I conclude this discourse,
Surrounded by water and metaphors,
With an old islander's good advice.
Go, seek your island;
Or, if you are an island,
Welcome explorers, offer food and water
And a small safe harbor
However temporary.

But remember:
An island is entire unto itself!
So, keep nearby
A log or raft or boat or, lacking these,
At least just learn to swim.

Zen

"What is Zen?" I'm asked,
And when I give an answer
Based on the little I know,
It's too simple,
And the questioner leaves feeling cheated.
Of course I know what it isn't.
It's not an excuse to wear sandals
And a beard and skip the soap.
In fact, it's not an excuse for anything!
Zen, I believe, is simply this:
An unquenchable thirst for truth
And the sure belief that only somewhere in the innerspace
Of self
Can truth ever be found.
The search is never easy,
For it requires the siphoning off
Of superfluous thought
And distillation of the residue—
And this, in turn, refined through sieves
Of concentration
Until the jewel lights the darkest corner
In the caverns of the mind.
Zen is the training that helps find the way.
Sitting, facing the wall in noble state,
Upright and serene, the lotus . . .
Not meditating, but tuning the mind to infinity—
So deep a concentration that hallucinations
Try to distract;
Apparitions tease and voices call,
But this is just a passing thing demanding a firm grip

On the handrail of one's discipline
And an emptying of the mind
To let the truth come rushing in.
A teacher helps,
For he has found the way.
And yet your search is quite alone—
Through the maze of koans
Set to nudge you into cosmic consciousness
With life and death perception . . .
What is the sound of one hand clapping?
Who were you before you were born?
This is no pre-chewed religion
And there is no way to cheat.
For you are there, inside yourself,
Looking, seeking . . .
And, if you hold the jewel,
You are the center of the universe.
Zen
Is a do-it-yourself kit of complete understanding
Of who you are, who you were, why you are
And what you'll be.
Without books—
For all is written in the wind.
Without pomp—
For the cathedral lies within you.
Without logic—
For only beyond the restricting bars of logic
Can truth be found:
The way of being born again.

Phone Call

Brrrrrrr! . . .
Brrrrrrr! . . .
Brrrrrrr! . . .
Brr.
Hello . . .?
Yes, speaking . . .
Oh, God . . . yes . . .?
God who . . .?
Oh. Just God,
With a capital "G."
Yes, what can I do for you . . .?
What can you do for me?
Oh, I see.
Well, for a start, explain yourself . . .
What's that? . . . Yes, I know I should . . .
Yes, I've read the book.
But, God, honestly, I'd like to read
It all, but that so-and-so begat
So-and-so jazz bugs me . . .
You've called to give me your grace . . .?
Great, I'd like that!
For you have watched my life and feel I deserve . . .
No, this is not HO 4-6429. This
Is HO 4-63 . . . What's that . . .?
Sorry, Wrong number!

The Poetry of Sex

"There he goes again,"
You say.
"Possessed by sex,
Obsessed by sex."
Why not?
There's very little in this world
With sex not at its root.
We form our own opinion of sex,
As we do of art and literature,
At quite an early age
And decide if it's to be a beast with two backs,
Or a being with two hearts;
Whether it's to be a veldt to hunt
For trophies on our wall,
Or a series of couplings,
Grunted from track to track;
Or a timid urge that must be gratified
At the expense of our conscience;
Or we learn the poetry of sex,
The rhythm, the beauty and the truth—
The heart-stopping awareness of the surge of living;
The interplay of moods,
The savage or the tender imagery of love:
The poetry of sex.

How sad that after all the years of thinking Man,
The worst swear word we've come up with
To express our disgust or anger
Is that great four-letter word
With which to vent our spleen:

Fuck!
And this word is also used by some
To describe the poetry of sex.
But, then too, as if in opposition to this,
Some say that they were "making love"—
In many cases a lie,
For love, so many times, is absent,
Though friendship fills the bed.
And making love is enough a happening
When it's true;
And when it's not, it makes the truth a creaking lie.
What can we call it then? What's in a name?
What semantic rose could be sweet enough
For this so sweet success?
Sex?
Yes.
But wait. Sex too is a bawdy bar,
A stripper's jut,
A hotel room rented by the hour,
A map of Australia staining the sheet,
Pawing hands, feelings, and fiddlings,
Rutting with the husband's key inside the lock,
Breastless whores lined up for choosing,
The pimply experimenters,
The furtive readers, thumbing through the girly magazines,
The call girls on the showroom carpet,
The rapist and the heavy breathing uncle
Giving candy to the little girl;
The dog and the old maid, the donkey and the girl.

Sex is dirty songs and dirty jokes
And the office party with the loaded drinks
Intended to lubricate the secretaries small divide.
It's man to man resuscitation of the libido,

Or woman to woman escape
From the icy world of men.

Sex is breasts and balls and thrusting tongues
And acrobatics around the gear shaft—
A Ford in your future.
What then is the alchemy
That makes this base metal
And transmutes it into the poetry of sex?

I think it's simply this:
Sex needs no label,
For it is too many things, too many ways,
Too many meanings.
Call it what you will,
At worst it's a three-letter word;
At best, it's poetry.
There is a necessary rhythm.
By this I don't mean tempo,
But the meter of the poem—
The quick bright there-will-never-be-tomorrow,
Or the cadence of the lingering shadows on the wall,
Or the total immersion that
Erases drafts or sirens or imperfections of the flesh,
Answering for the moment
All the questions of the mind.

The hair spread on the pillow,
Dark as seaweed, or bright as a spin of gold—
Long hair wrapped around you,
Over you, under you—
A fragrant rope to haul you out of now.
Hands clutching, clenching, caressing,
Or spread out to be crucified

With gutty spikes of passion;
Or scooping up the ecstacy as it flows.
Long, slim fingers tipped with many thousand volts—
Soft touches borrowing stolen time—
Cool, caressing,
Making it hard
To resist the feel,
If not the fact, of love.

Breasts,
Little curves, tip-tilted;
Confections, cherry-tipped
Or salty presumptions with hard black olives
Thrusting up—
Ripe fruits, overflowing,
Only fully appreciated when above you—
When supine, dumplings boiling over.

Sweet breasts tipped with ginger,
Roused by kisses
And, always, one a little bigger than
The other—
Cool breasts, warmed by a flush
That comes as she comes,
Softened by shadows, moved by rhythm,
Arched or relaxed or taut as bows,
The heart-stopping perfection of her
Geometry.

Legs, dancing to the music set by circumstance,
Holding, guiding.
The lover's triangle
That needs the "open sesame"
Of desire to unlock the way to all its hidden poetry;

Soft as love itself, unquenchable as deserts,
Bottomless as thought; sometimes a fleshy trap
From which there is no escape;
Sometimes a dream from which there's no awakening.

The eyes, the nose,
The triggering ears,
The warm intoxication of the neck,
The belly with its simple dimple
And the reverse—
Two curves,
Each a reflection of the other moon,
Eclipsed when sat upon.

All this and more
Of sex's Thesaurus.
And of the scene itself—
Why, this depends entirely on the need,
The urgency, or whim—
Not only of the poets,
But of the meld of circumstance,
With patience the alliteration.
Woman needs her poetry double-spaced,
But when the rhythms match
Then comes the rhyme without the reasons—
The thousand violins and all that jazz—
The sneeze that says, "God bless you,"
The long, high scream of wonder,
The flashing lights,
The tilt,
The rush of self into self of fusion—
Cha cha cha.
And then, the coda—
The repeat of wonder riding wonder piggyback—

The spiral back to now again—
The only way to fly—
The little instant sadness—
The poetry of sex.

Cat

A cat
Looked out of the past one day,
Then slid from out of a tree,
Shook off the Pharaoh's dust
And stalked an ancient enemy.
Through the grove of memory
It arched its back to a
Poisoned wind
And slanted its eyes to the
Moon.
And then, this ancient, evil
Egyptian cat,
Did a big shit on my best carpet!

Sneeze

A sneeze
Unsneezed,
Welling up
Tantalizingly exquisite,
Excruciatingly near
And yet unsneezed,
Suddenly explodes!
Bringing ecstasy
And cliff-hung relief
And boundless joy
All in the same microsecond:
Just like an orgasm!

———

God bless you!

Letter to a Teen-Age Daughter

My Darling:
   I haven't seen you since you were five
   And I know you'd not appreciate
   Mental pictures of you chubby on a rug
   In that lifetime when I knew you.
   We enjoyed walks and bathtime tickling
   And stories.
   And I still have photographs
   Of that little girl you used to be.
   But that was then
   And now you are a woman, almost,
   And I would lie if I told you I know you,
   Or can imagine how you tick.
   Your picture shows me
   A hip and happy girl;
   Your letters, too,
   Tell me you've kept two gifts
   I wished on you when you were born:
   A sense of humor and a lust for life.
   And to this I know you've added
   All your mother's charm and grace.

   The gap between the baby girl
   And the you, now self-possessed,
   Flashed by me.
   I didn't go through your growing up . . .
   The cuts, the bumps,
   The up and down succession of your school days,
   The badges and awards,
   The losses and the gains,

The dabs of clay experience
Now molded into you.
I didn't see you fill out
Physically and mentally . . .
Now I have a woman,
Way across the world,
Who is differently
A part of me.

I'm sure you must have asked
Why I left you and went off into the world
Only linked by letters
And a chain of checks for
Alimony and child support.
I did it for so many reasons . . .
So important then and unimportant now.
But, I must add, with no regrets.
For you will find,
Now that you are a woman,
That we do what we must do
And, in the decisions, right or wrong,
An inch right or an inch left,
Or a second earlier,
Cannot be calculated
And the decimal points
Fall where they may.
I abandoned you only on paper
For, in my heart, I've agonized
Over your sicknesses and your struggles
To peck out of your shell.
I've applauded everything you've done
That's clever and funny
And now you're completely
The way I hoped you'd be.

Your mother lost me and, in doing, gained.
And all she's done for you
Can't be assessed,
But this is sure:
She architected you
With such loving care,
From firm foundation
To your twinkling symmetry,
That you will never stand vacant,
But will house the myriad wonders
Of this, our funny life.
I want to meet you, yet
I fear the meeting.
For a paper father
Has a certain mystery.
I pop up on post cards from Japan,
In gifts from Europe,
Mail from Spain.
I do no wrong
In all my scribbled words,
But I'm not paper.
Or, if I am,
You'd find I'm covered with so many words and pictures,
So many doodles, so many crossings out,
So many foldings, creasings, blots, and errors
That I wonder,
Will you accept me as I am—
As I accept the girl inside my wallet?
Somehow, I think you will.
And, if you do,
What a triumph of transition!
What a very marvelous,
Marvelous,
Thing . . .

Anatomy of a Marriage

The marriage knot is not a noose,
But if the rope is tied too loose
It tends to tangle.
While stretched around the necks of kin
It's also apt to strangle.
Would you mind awfully if I slip out of rhyme
And into something more comfortable?
Thanks.
This is too touchy a subject
To touch with flippancy,
So I'll take my tongue out of my cheek
And speak my mind about that most awesome masquerade—
The Act of Marriage.
If marriages are indeed made in Heaven
The gods must stuff their mouths full of clouds
To stop from laughing
At the absurdities they see below.
And now, one more procrastination
Before I plunge a pick or two into this sacred cow,
For both my editor and publisher (both married)
State that all opinions expressed herein
Are my own
And they are not responsible for my audacity
Or my alimony.
Now . . .
This cat, "A," meets this chick, "B,"
And, at some point of madness,
Decides that she is the only woman in the world
And marries her, okay?
Why? How does he know? How many has he tried?

Has he checked out other sizes, models, and colors?
And if the answer's "yes," why only two or three?
Why not a regular Masters-Johnson sampling?
How does he know
That next year, next week, next day he won't find
The superduper Kewpie doll
With the gen-yew-wine ring a ding ding?
He doesn't know, does he?
OK, Miss "B" has saved her sweet, unstretched virginity
(Marked 'V')
When, suddenly, she decides to give it away to Mr. "A,"
In return for a few mumbles in church.
How does she know that he doesn't need
A psychiatrist more than a wife,
Or that she won't be forced
To play the role of Rex's mother all her life?
She doesn't know, does she?
All right, All right, I hear you.
Right, let's say that Mr. "A" and Miss "B"
Decide, against all the television codes,
To give it a dry run; run it up the flagpole
And see who salutes,
See how the cookie crumbles before they post the bans.
And say, it's like crazy, like wow, like Getz—
Like it's too good for the peasants.
They've got it made, or have they?
Any bets?
Well, have they? Come on, stop huffing and burping.
You're right, they might or they might not.
Right?
For to ask two people to endure
The daily constant shock of discovering the incredible
Things that make their mates tick
Is too much.

Those moments of horror as they watch
The one they chose—damn it!—
Do things that make their mental toes curl up
And hear the words come out of that sweet-kissed mouth
Like little pearls of poison.
Or worse, to feel a sickening gush of pity
Come rushing over them like warm glue. It's so frightening
That they're torn between hara-kiri
And a quick stab with the paper knife.

There will now be a short intermission for all the
Happily married couples to coo, "Not us, not us!
Not me!"
Well, wait. To the small, select elite,
Those married couples so stupid, or so intelligent
That their marriage is a thing of beauty and a joy—
This I must agree:
Armed with a boundless sense of humor,
Blessed with a certain deafness,
A governor of dumbness
And a rigidly controlled curiosity,
It can and does work—
As witnessed by the population explosion,
The his-and-her credit cards
And dual-control electric blankets.
However, the strongest mortar in the Great Wall of Marriage
Is compromise.
So, he's not a knight in shining armor; he's kind.
So, she's not built like a brick outhouse; she's intelligent.
So, he's not a genius; he's reliable.
So, she's not built like a brick outhouse;
Well, I can dream, can't I?

How cruel to suggest

That dreams come between people in bed.
How perverted to suggest
That Mrs. "A" thinks Mr. "A" is making love to her
While, really, he's pleasuring a gatefold in relief
While she amplifies his humble efforts
Into Rock or Ringo or Omar—
Depending on her age or mood or depth of her imagination.
And, too often, a bed's a place to lie in.
How many women, this very night, will lie awake,
Unquenched
While their hero, having proved himself to himself,
Rolls over and plays dead?
How many men tonight will lie with wretched heart
Because they didn't make it,
And wonder if they ever will again,
Ashamed of their inadequacy and puzzled
By the headaches suffered by their suffering wives
Between the curlers and the cold cream and the
Frozen wastes of bed?
They both forget that "talk" is also a four-letter
Word describing intercourse
And without the give and take of it,
Pride's a leaky condom
And life has no conception.
As for infidelity—
It's a strange, biological fact
That a man's ego is situated some nine inches
Below his navel.
While a woman's ego
Lies beneath her ivory domes and deep within
Her heart.

Oh, come on. You know I'm putting you on again.
Marriage is great . . .

Well, if it's a giving thing it has a chance
And can be full of chances pattering round the house.
If it's an honest thing, it has a prayer
And, in its answering, resounds a great "Amen."
For marriage is the old math of loneliness—
The need to have and to hold a someone of one's own,
The urge to seek a permanence,
A sounding board for our emotions
And, if the unimportant things are made important,
The remembering, the flowers,
The resisting of any impulse to put the other down;
The giving and the warming,
Then all the other things
Resolve themselves to memories
In the scrapbook of the heart.
So there . . .
Despite my cynicism, I've come on strong
For good old rice and orange blossoms
For, after all,
Anything that's a tax deduction can't be all bad,
Can it?

Psychedelia

Here, in the black back of my mind,
Colors wait to be squeezed
On monochromatic memories,
Faded by time,
Bleached by suns and moons,
Exposed by lightning flashes . . .
Flash!
Flash!
Bazam!
Zap!
Red . . .
Bloody red,
Blood red,
Better dead than red.
Pins in pomegranates,
Raspberry ice and squashed tomatoes
Splotch!
The gurkha's kukri!
Makes a crimson flower bloom
Where the bullock's head once lowed . . .
Crack!
Good show!
The red planet leaves the bat;
Well caught!
Howzat!
The slip swished to the floor
And then the carmine petticoat . . .
Ahhhh . . .
Wheeeee, the siren sounds
And how we ran to watch the hose unwind

And feel the flames turning our cheeks to fire . . .
Beside you,
In your red, quilted dressing gown,
And one more log
Before we add our shadows to the flickering . . .
The rose, a throb of blood above the thorn
And, in the candle light,
The wine, still and ceremonious.
The guard's parade—a thin red line
And blood, a blurring mass of red,
Rimmed with flies a darker red.
Kung hey fat choy! New Year . . .
And lipstick lingering on a
Pillow . . . red, for danger . . .
Red,
Head,
Said,
Bed.
And now the yellow candlelight
Casts us adrift in a sea of darkness,
All alone on a yellow sea.
And take your Atabrine, you fool,
Or else you'll look like me.
She wore a yellow *cheong-sam* . . .
Her yellow skin
Like ivory there in the yellow
Hotel room in Nathan Road,
Soft in the yellow dawn.
I wandered lonely as a cloud
"I know it, sir. I do! I do!"
When all at once I saw a crowd . . .
And what a noble fruit
The lemon is: the heart of summer.
Tenderizing meat, perking drinks,

Deodorizing fish,
Adding fragrance to salads,
Subtlety to puddings,
And even once, scooped out,
A contraceptive!
Oh, Lord! My saffron gown
And begging bowl
Say more than all my prayers.
And in that sordid room
The little bunch of primroses looked like hope,
Its cord still tied,
And time waits for no one. As the signals change,
Is it the same idiot who always sounds his horn?
Red . . .
Yellow . . .
A tisket, a tasket,
You're green, my little basket . . .
Lime cool,
Lush leaves,
Long lanes awash with springtime;
Green dawns and apples hanging;
Melons in rows
And, above,
Her eyes across the table:

Cats, and dime store manicure:
Green claws of Frankenstein.
Green beans and green jeans,
Two more melons moving.
Green depths beneath the diving board.
Go . . .
Go safely green in large denominations.
Green, the smell of gangrene,
Tangerine,

Tangiers,
Algiers:
The sun up there, a beach ball thrown
Above the orange beach.
Bitch!
Orange hair and smile, like marmalade in bed,
Bitter-sweet and sticky.
Note: To prevent pregnancy
Drink orange juice.
Before or after?
No, instead! Ha, ha.

Orange juice,
Orange jokes,
Orange juice sorry that you made me cry?
Knock knock who's there?
Only us oranges, full of pith and juice,
And nothing rhymes with orange . . .
Not even sugar.
Wham!
Bam!
Alakazam!
Under an orange-colored sky.
Blue, azure blue,
Blue.
True blue, as blue as the spot
On an Asian baby's bum.
And my trim blue uniform;
My RAF-ish background,
My half wing in the wild, blue yonder.
I see the mountains of the moon,
Craggy with shadows,
Cooling wildebeest
With edges shaky in the midday heat,

Far from the sea,
Posing for post cards.
And that blue linen dress you wore
That let your nipples show like pips.
And that night you were my blue girl;
I teased you as you wept blue tears
And I kissed you there in that blue place
Where I could look up and see
Your breasts . . .
The mountains of the moon.
And somewhere a noodle vender's horn
Blew a blue note that hit me in the spine.
Blue haze,
Hazy,
Crazy,
Tickled pink.
Purple prunes,
Pruned people.

Silver slivers,
Gold,
Gilt,
Guilty gold,
Ghelt,
God . . .

Candyfloss prayers and lollypop books;
White Christmas, white Christians,
Black Muslims, black muslin,
Crepe,
Crap

For when I lay me down to die,
Color me gone.

The Jungle

A river twists
And flashes back an insult at the sun
For revealing its escape route to the sea,
For it contrives to snake unnoticed
Through the jungle hills.
The jungle, from the air, looks kind enough
With verdant greens packed close together
And all the wildness of parsley edge to edge—
Here and there a clearing and the flash of shining water,
But for hours and hours one sees only the sea of green.

From below, the jungle is a very different thing.
First, it's old—
Old as time and very, very wise,
Filled with instincts for its protection
Multiplied a million times.
A jungle finds more ways to repel intruders
Than all the survival manuals tell.
They range from simple death to emerald madness—
Not from snakes or beasts,
Who much prefer to go their way in peace,
But by thirst
With a river just over the hill,
Or exhaustion by the trick of hypnotism
Or by fever, or a thousand other jungle wiles,
For she, the forest, has a way of closing in.
A sudden silence as the birds are stilled—
The monkey stops his chattering—
The sky, a distant disc above the trees, spins faster—
Then, the awful knowledge that this charade

Is the first syllable of an endless word—
A pantomime of death.

But, oh! There's beauty in the jungle—
Enough to stop the heart and eye.
Greens not seen except in dreams
And statues carved to decorate
Cathedrals pillared with fluted trees
And stained glass windows in the wings
Of secret birds and butterflies.

And tigers lie,
Long pink tongues panting—
Sunlight and shadow—
Dreaming of whatever tigers dream
As they lie dozing in the thicket's heat,
Savoring the little breeze that cools their ruff
Down where the river swirls.
And the other creatures too
Slip through the bars of the forest floor
And eat and are eaten according to their role.
And, rarely too,
Some kind of man lives in the jungle and survives—
Not by fighting it,
But by accepting age-old Nature's laws.

But now the jungle shelters horror never planned by Nature—
Booby traps, Claymore mines,
Tunnels, guns, and desperate men.
And death, not for food or instinct's savagery,
But for a reason
The jungle's heard so many, many times before
And will again,
Until she covers up the scars—

Grows over bones and bayonets,
Shrouds the armless, legless bodies
With a new, green funeral robe;
Erases camps and airstrips
And forgets
The awful things men do to one another.

The Sea

I have seen the sea in many moods
And felt its presence
Even though miles away from it.
I have no Mansfield love for it
And feel no lure to be alone by it.
Nor do I hear its call.
And yet,
The more you think of it—
The sea, I mean—
The more it stirs that tiny itch
Inside your brain—
That "almost" understanding of all the reasons why—
Of why we are
And why the sea should be.

On the surface, the sea reflects emotions
Easily reproduced by Kodak—
Lovers' dreams and poets' pens.
Sequined seas,
Jade green between
The mainland and Hong Kong;
The wine dark seas—if wine is blue—
Between the islands of the gods;
Frothy seas and frisky seas
And seas with saber teeth;
The queasy heavy heaving sea
Scratching its hoary back against the rocks of Scotland;
The sparkling seas, skittering sunshine
And the silver-paper seas
With palm trees—pasted silhouettes;

Melancholy seas that stretch to infinity
And mewky, pewky seas
Lapping up rubbers and orange peels
And belching 'neath the pier;
The brisk, bright sea
With ostrich feathers curling down its cleavage;
And seas so deep that auld lang syne
Sinks like a stone into its depths.

The children's sea, squealingly exciting
And full of slippery wiggles,
Always there to touch-you-last—
A handy, sloshing, joshing plaything
That doesn't have to be tidied up or put away—
Bucketable and splashable,
Marred only by its icky taste.

The sailors' sea,
Predictable in its unpredictability,
Charted and yet untouched,
Despite a million keels
And the discipline of countless rudders.
Not cruel, for cruelty needs a reason;
Not compassionate,
For compassion needs a depth of understanding.
The sea—
A tool for sailors' trade.

The lovers' sea—
A background for honeymoons,
A cadence for passion,
A chance to play Canute,
A thing to sit and look at
While you dream of other things.

And yet it's not romantic,
For romance needs sex for a carrot
To lead it on its merry way.
Not that the sea is sexless—
Heaven knows it writhes
With couplings so complex,
So intricate,
That a piscatorial Kama Sutra
Would be on such a scale
As to give all landlubbers
A dry and arid complex,
Even without contemplating
The copulation of the whale!

Down!
Down!
Down!
Under the skin of wave and flotsam—
Green, black ooze
And there is the past—
The very womb of man—
A hole in space—
Filled with Pandora's box of goodies,
The sustenance of life,
The richness undredged,
The answers to questions as yet unasked.
And yet—
Up,
Up,
Up,
Through the turbulence and jetsam,
Through the fruit of plankton to the surface—
Blue,
Bright beneath the moon

Or boiling bent on cold destruction
Or sullenly shouldering the land.

The sea,
Described by metaphors
Or onomatopoetic phrases,
Conjuring visions,
Evoking songs and symphonies,
Described in every way but wet.
The sea—
A *koan* without words;
The quintessence of philosophy.
For if you see the sea
And look away
And then look back,
The sea you see
Is not the same sea you saw—
Or, if you prefer,
The sea you saw
Is not the same sea
You see.

Cobber

If I had to fight,
And have an ally on my flank,
I'd pick an Aussie.
For you never hear a word against them,
Except in bars,
Where they're inclined to pick a Sheila for themselves
And charm her to exclusiveness.

The Aussies have a knack of balancing
Tough, rough, ruthlessness
With outback arid humor
And a way of improvising
So, that, even in a war—
Where the jungle constitutes the greatest enemy—
You'll find the Aussie quite at home.

And when they die—as die they do,
For they're always in the thick of things—
At Heaven's gate they'll slouch right in
And slap St. Peter on the back
With "Good-day, mate. How are you?"
As friendly as can be.
And St. Peter, good soul as he is,
Will get up from the ground
And show the digger where to brew his tea.

Yes, if I had to fight
And have an ally by my side,
I'd pick an Aussie.
And, in reports,

You just don't hear enough about them.
For they're inclined to slip out of the jungle
And turn into the big, raw-boned guy there at the bar
Who damns the local beer
And, swearing towering, bloody oaths,
Shoots through into the night.

Snowman

A snowman
Lies on an army cot
With only seeping blood to show
A human being fights for life
Beneath the snowy bandage shroud.

The snowman has only one leg
And his eyes, when he can bear to open them,
Reveal the horror that he knew
When he found himself deprived,
By one sharp blow,
Of leg,
Of future dreams,
Of wholeness,
And the chance to be a boy again.

No leg to slide and touch the base with,
No leg to press down on the gas and make the buggy leap with,
No leg to frug or swim or twine with
Nylon legs in darkened rooms.
No chance to look back on the war
As an adventure or an episode,
Half-forgotten in the chore of catching up with life again.
The snowman closes bruised eyes
And melts to kind unconsciousness.

In the End

I'd like to meet the man
Who cut latrine holes in Bien Hoa,
For his four-seaters
Deprive one of the comfort
Conducive to good morning
Conversation with one's neighbors
Or the perusal of a magazine,
Let alone the joy of just sitting there—
Contemplating.

It's not the fact that I object
To rural inconvenience,
For plumbing in the field
Is often crude,
Especially in the rear.
But these Bien Hoa commodes
Are the unkindest cut of all—
Not fit design nor designed to fit—
Ensuring only one sure thing:
Clients all leave with the same impression.

Purple Heart

My marriage is a good one,
Filled with simple, splendid things
One looks for, dreams of,
And sometimes takes for granted—
The warmth of coming home,
The pleasuring of sharing,
Even the warm backside so welcome in a winter bed.

My marriage is not old enough
To take for granted the powerful dynamo of sex
That makes the days hum by
And fills the nights with sparks
And funny, lustful things
That, shared, become a surging poetry.

At first we couldn't believe
That I would have to go,
That she would, from here on in, sleep alone
In our double bed,
And that I would only touch her now
With letters from Viet Nam.

On the last night—
By that I mean the night before I left—
She lay in my arms,
Her hair a darker shadow,
Her eyes catching the moonlight
From the open window—gauzy curtains
Ballooning a little in the midnight breeze.
"Darling," she said

In that special after-sex voice of hers,
"Take care, you hear?"
What could I say?
Yes, sure I will . . . or more inane . . . you bet!
And so, instead, I kissed her
And already felt the stirrings
As her breast pressed against my hand.
"Darling," she said again,
"Those women over there . . .
Be careful. I hear they're beautiful
And you'll be gone a year."
I stopped her there and then

And kissed the salt soup of her eyes
And gently stroked her into readiness.

As she sang her little cries of love
I stopped above her and I said
"You're the only girl I need—now and forever."
She pulled me down to her
And the truth seemed simple and complete.
But that was long ago—
A long, tedious, journey ago—
A pyramid, of burning months in Viet Nam,
Ago.

And now, my love, what can I say?
Where is the truth, so simple and complete?
Not in my letters that I signed, "with all my love . . ."
Not in the hours before I slept and tried
And tried to see her face—
Not when I teased myself, reviving erotic memories
Of her beneath me, above me, beside me—
Not when I read her letters, feeling an imposter

Reading thoughts not meant for me.
The truth is simply this:
The first few months I learned to survive,
Not just from Charlie, but from officers and NCO's
Who put the fear of God in me—
Far worse than the hidden enemy.
I found myself knowing where to be and where not to be,
How to go along
And make the things I didn't have work for me
And make the senselessness around me make sense sometimes.
Of course I thought of sex.
Who didn't?
Though the village near the base was out of bounds
Some of the men sneaked out and took their chances.
I wasn't even tempted,
Though I'll admit I lay with *Playboy* and I hope
The Playmate of the Month will never know
What stimulating company she provided
On the long, hot lonely nights.
But actual sex—no.
Not that it would have mattered I guess.
For, to a man, sex can sometimes be just that
With only passing conscience giving nothing, taking little,
And altering little in the balance of his life.

A shuffle found me posted to Saigon.
I went to bars and cabarets with Jack.
Remember Jack from Barney Brothers?
He took a whirl shacking up with a most spectacular bar girl
Who specialized in setting up house.
Not one night stands but arrangements more substantial.
It worked out fine till, one week later,
Jack got pretty sick
And canceled the contract

And, sadder but a little wiser,
Became a Saigon bachelor again.
I sat with girls and talked to them,
Mostly for the comfort of being with someone soft again
After the sweaty harshness of my roommates.
When one of the girls suggested bed
I showed my wife's photo and, this way,
We became good friends and nothing more,
And I enjoyed my evening visits with the chance
Of buying myself a beer and the little girl a glass of tea,
Despite the $2 tab for it.
Looking back, I felt secure
And the days were passing fast.
I even felt that I'd survive the war without a scratch;
Come home without a wound.

I met Ba—
That's the only name I knew her by.
She told me the rest the first night I met her.
She laughed like a little silver bell when
I tried to repeat it.
"Just call me Ba," she said. And so I did.
Ba is nineteen
And so slim of waist and wrist
That kids at school would call her skinny.
Ba left school when she was twelve
And helped her mother until she died and left her
In the dubious care of an uncle who tried to seduce her
And keep her as an unpaid maid.
She ran away and French sisters cared for her and,
When she left them
To seek work, the boss of a rice store locked her in his room
And only her screams, which brought the bastard's wife,
Saved her once again.

And now, she worked in this small bar—
The only girl, it seemed, who lived off the percentage
From the tea
And didn't make the short-time scene,
Or shack up with some NCO
And salt away part of his monthly pay.
A virgin in a Saigon bar? That's what she told me.
I was not naïve enough to believe it all at first,
But more and more I found myself going to her place
And sitting there, oblivious to the drunks and jukebox,
Content to drink my drink and sit and talk
In the darkest corner to my little virgin, Ba.
I told her about my home, my wife, America,
And we communicated with her little English
And my little French,
And a little Vietnamese dictionary
I'd bought after my third visit.
Ba—
I wish you could see her. She stood just heart high,
Her little face an oval framed by hair so black,
So long, so soft, so scented—maybe the way Eve's hair
Had tempted Adam.
Her hands were small with long curved nails
And her body slim, but blossoming to pointed breasts
Accented by her *ao-dai* with its Chinese collar
And close-fitting bodice.
Her legs, in matching satin trousers,
Long and shapely as she walked.
Her skin so soft and blemish-free.
But it was the eyes you must try and visualize—
Her eyes were . . . How can I describe them?
Were bright, as if a little lamp inside shone out.
They were the eyes of a women and yet,
The innocence of a child was there—

Quick to smile and quick to cry,
Not a trace of bar girl hardness,
Not a glint of commercial cunning—
The eyes of a virgin—
The eyes of Ba.

Slowly, I became eager to visit her
And always found her waiting there in our corner
As if she'd combed her straight black hair
And waited just for me.
I reasoned that the reason for her availability
Was that all the guys had tried
And, getting nowhere, had moved on to more rewarding girls
Who sought their just reward.
About this time, I fell in love with Ba.
The first time I admitted it to myself I felt absurd,
For it was such an obvious thing to do,
Such an old story:
Man away from home, lonely,
Attractive girl, exotic surroundings.
And yet, I reasoned that love is
A set of circumstances bringing two people together—
An antidote for man's eternal loneliness,
A state of mind aided by the physical wonder
Of being male and female.
Love is not semantics, but a certain chemistry
Of time and space and need—
The cause and effect of being human.

I fell in love with Ba.
I felt myself sweating as I thought of her.
Not the hot sweat of a Viet Nam Sunday,
But the cold sweat of wonder, the quickening heart,
The eager breath, the phenomenon of love.

Then it struck me—of course!
My ego yearned for conquest!
Here was this girl, this child, belonging to no one,
Possessed by no one.
And here was I, far enough from home to be in another world,
And with the constant itch I couldn't scratch.
And now good sense won through—
My marriage was a good one filled with the simple,
Splendid things,
And I was old fashioned enough—wasn't I?—
To believe in the sanctity of marriage
And brought up to believe adultry a sin.
But, still, I found myself in love with Ba.
So I stayed away from her.
I wrote long letters home
And told my wife the daily trivia—all the aggravations,
And signed each letter
"As always, all my love . . ."

Ba fell in love with me about this time.
She told me
I'd not been near and she had feared that I had gone away,
But she sat waiting in our corner
In hopes that I might come.
I came this night because I felt a fool
For making too much of what was happening
And argued, why deny myself the harmless pleasure?
After all, in a month and two days, I'd be going home.
After those first few minutes when she shyly told me
That she loved me,
I teased her and asked her why.
She looked at me and held my hand and gave me the only answer
A man needs to lose his reason—
Because, she said, "I've never known a man till now

Who makes me feel this way."
And with those lovely eyes filled to brimming
I felt my armor slip away
And the childish game of being in love
Came back to me as
If it were yesterday—
The hay rides, the kissing in the park,
The ache, the joy,
The quickening of the clumsy nerves
That makes you spill things and forget the time.
I sat starry-eyed; a man, a boy again,
Enthralled by a little princess
Sipping tea from a shot glass
And looking at me as if I were God.
And I feeling so mortal
I couldn't wait to put my arms around her
And, if need be, fight the ten marines
Who bickered by the bar.

I didn't ask her to sleep with me,
But, somehow, found myself in a cheap hotel room
With Ba beside me on the bed.
She was dressed in a sheath of shadows
And her long, black hair enfolded us.
I cradled her in my arms,
Content to feel her close to me.
Her breasts were fuller than I'd dreamed
And lay heavy, soft in my loving hand.
Her breath was sweet.
I kissed the corners of her mouth.
Her eyes, the soft curve of her throat, her shoulders,
And down until her nipples hardened in my mouth.
I touched a spring inside of her,
For now she turned onto her back and stretched herself.

And I could feel the rhythm of her breathing quicken.
From passiveness she came alive—
She moved and moaned and pulled me closer
And I, ready, but unwilling to take the plunge;
To—what do they say?—despoil the flower.
She ground herself against me,
Screamed and struggled, shuddered so
That, for a while, I feared she'd stop and run away.
But still she pressed
And I, with all thoughts of chivalry long gone,
Began the long crescendo
To match the music of her mood.
She arched her back, her breasts taut.
Impatiently, she pulled me to her and then I heard the
Words she said:
"Jazz me, you mother! Jazz me good!
Screw me, baby! Go! Go! Go!"
It was too late for me to stop.
I screwed her with a savagery—a man possessed—
All love forgotten and, when I was done,
I lay exhausted.
But my little virgin moaned for more,
Her English clear with its "Deep South" drawl.

I came out of my dream and shook my head.
Was it all a lie, or just a part of it?
The uncles and nuns and the rice man's wife?
Why pick me and what was the reason?
I'll never know, not all my life.

The men she'd known have all gone home
And left behind their words for her
And taken with them secret dreams
Their hearts intact and ego shining.

Back to their families, back to their wives,
Even as I would return to mine.

On that last night—
By that I mean the last night in Viet Nam—
She lay in my arms, her hair a darker shadow,
Her eyes catching the moonlight from the open window.
"Oh," she said
In that little after-sex voice of hers,
"Will you come back?"
What could I say?
Of course I will? or worse, no, never?
So, instead I kissed her
And again felt the stirring of her breasts
Pressed against my chest.
She said, "Your wife . . . you love her?
You soon forget? You not remember Ba?"
I stopped her there and then and kissed her dry, wise eyes
And gently touched the secret places
Where the dragon of her passion lay.
And, as she crooned her crude love patter,
I stopped awhile above her and looked down.
"I won't forget you, Ba," I said
And, as she pulled me down and into her,
The truth seemed simple and complete.

Next day I climbed aboard a plane
And, as it rose sharply from the runway
To avoid stray shots from some ambitious Charlie
In the paddy fields below,
I looked down at Saigon
Spread 'neath the speeding jet's wide wings.
I tried to spot the hotel where we'd lain,
But from so high the buildings blurred together

And soon disappeared.
And there was just the shining sea
Between me and all my dreams of home.

A Grunt's Prayer

Oh Lord,
Another day has ended
And I thank you
For not revealing
To the other guys
How scared I am.

It's not so much
The fear of being killed,
As the horror
Of winding up
Like Pete—
Poor bastard—
Without legs.
Or like Colin who
Will always live
(If it is living)
In darkness and in pain.

I thank you, Lord,
For giving me the will
To do as I'm told,
While every fiber
Of my being rebels
And wants to run away—
Away from all the awful sounds of war
And the relentless pour of sand
In the hourglass of my life.
Lord, too, I thank you
For the strength you give me

And the sometime mental block
That shuts out
The cries, the screams,
Of friend and foe,
And that seditious voice
That cries within me.

For those at home—
Lord,
Be kind with time
And fill their hours so full of it
That days will blur to weeks,
Weeks to months,
And then be gone
To be replaced by days more easily understood.

For my mother—
Bless her.
Lord, let her dream good dreams
And let the time that I'm away
Touch her only gently.
And let her greatest concern be
That I use the powder that she sends
To put between my toes
And that I change my shorts.
And, Lord, please—
Just give me time
To get it over with,
To do what I must.
And forgive me, please,
For breaking your commandments—
For, if I obey You,
Then I am dubbed a coward—
Or worse, a traitor.

And, if I obey my leaders,
Then I must kill
Or be killed.
So please
Give me the faith to believe
That any sin approved
By Act of Congress
Finds absolution
And I,
A state of grace
Before my Lord
—Amen

The Roundabout

We ride the roundabout,
Our penny paid
By some unthanked philanthropist.
Round we go, round we go,
Merrily we hold the pole—
Rise and fall,
Drunk with the blaring calliope.
Our horse,
Our horse has flaring nostrils.
Its mane flies frozen in the wind.
It eyes are bold, fixed straight ahead,
Its saddle gold, its tassels red,
Its gallop carved in wide midstride,
Its dappled sides quite free from sweat.
Round we ride the roundabout,
The other horses syncronized—
Some rise, some fall, some prance ahead,
Some stay behind,
And some flank us as we ride.

Faster and faster whirls the sound,
The outside blurs, we hold on tight,
But now our mind imbues our horse with life—
Its sweaty flanks now steam,
Its nostrils snort,
Its bloodshot eyes roll wildly in its head.

Now is the time
To let the reins flow through the hands
With careful sensitivity,

Or else the bit will cut our steed
And it may rear up on the pole
Which skewers it to the whirling roundabout.

We stare ahead,
But if you dare to tear away your gaze
You'll see the giddy, whirling mass—
The maelstrom around us,
The abyss beneath the skirting board.

And, as we slow,
The spinning space become the flaking paint,
The tinsel drapes, the chintzy signs.
Now some riders must dismount
And leave the golden roundabout
And stand there helpless,
Watching as it gathers speed again,
Whirling and spinning,
The riders crouched against the wind,
Faces aglow, looking ahead,
Forgetting that they're running in a circle,
Thinking the front lies straight ahead
And that they're riding wild and free
Covering a thousand leagues—
And not the roundabout's periphery.

As for me,
I'll wait until the ride creaks to a halt
And proffer up my secret penny
And ride again.
But I'll switch mounts,
For the horses, I've learned,
Are only made of wood,
But wow!

That unicorn is something else again—
I'll ride him,
Not just round and round,
But out into the stars.